MENTAL EQUITY
A Guide to Finding What You're Looking For

J. F. Lassiter II

Edited by Stephana Colbert

Cover Design by Michelle Claud

ISBN:
ISBN-13:

To my father and my namesake, who started me on this journey before I was old enough to even understand it.

To my mother, whose pride and belief in me propelled me through even my darkest days.

To my younger brother, for whom I wish to set the best example.

And finally, to my wife, my partner in life, who helped me conceive this project and stood by me throughout.

I love you all. Thank you.

TABLE OF CONTENTS

Preface

Thank you. The very first thing I want you to experience when you begin reading this book is my gratitude. I am grateful for your interest in this little book and the time you spend with it, whether it's minutes, hours or days.

Whether you decided to take a gander because you know me and want to share your support, are simply curious about its contents, or genuinely interested in finding what you are looking for, know that I appreciate you.

Don't worry; I know you didn't open this book over the millions of others just to read about why I wrote it. I promise you it is relevant, and it won't take very long. I felt compelled to write this book because I spent my entire life trying to figure out what I was looking for and how to find it. Does that make sense? If it doesn't now, it will very soon.

When my wife, then fiancée, a CPA, explained the definition of equity, I realized the concept could be applied to more than just finance. It could be applied to the way we look at life entirely.

Equity is the value of an asset minus the number of liabilities on that asset.

Now let's take that definition and apply it to life. If the liability is the effort we expend at work, in relationships or just life in general; and the asset is what we obtain with that effort, then the Equity is why we are really working. The joy that asset brings us and the justification for why we expel the effort for that particular asset results in fulfillment from obtaining a goal we worked for. This fulfillment is what I call **Mental Equity**.

Whether it's what we do or how we do it, we must meet our basic human needs first and foremost. If the work put into life does not afford us the basic needs, we all work for, then we are certainly not gaining joy from it. At that point, something must change.

Beyond our need for food and shelter, everyone is looking for something different. The guide that follows will help you find *your* something. It will help you accumulate your **Mental Equity**.

PART ONE

KNOW YOURSELF

"The two most important days in our lives are the day we are born and the day we find out why."
- Mark Twain

Before we can find what we are looking for, or even *know* what we are looking for, we must first know ourselves. The first and possibly the most difficult hurdle in knowing ourselves is being honest with ourselves and accepting who we are at the very core of our being. Learning to face ourselves means facing our deepest insecurities, vulnerabilities, and our darkest thoughts and desires. It means having the audacity to face our demons.

On the other hand, it means understanding what drives us, gets us out of bed in the morning, and motivates us to do the work. It means learning where our passions lie and what we are willing to fight for. Facing ourselves means realizing the duality of our character - our positive and negative traits - and balancing them. We will talk more about *duality* later in this book.

First, I'd like to share a bit of my own experience. I am a Virginia Tech graduate with a bachelor's degree in Packaging Systems and Design. My mother is a retired schoolteacher, and my father is a clinical psychologist.

The summer after graduation, I worked for a manufacturing company for about two months. I was let go because of my own lack of mindfulness. This unfortunate turn of events sent me spiraling toward my rock bottom. I had nobody to blame but

4

myself.

Completely lost, and sinking deeper into depression, I meandered through life for a while before going back home. Struggling to find purpose, I went to work in my father's clinic. It was less of a job and more of a safety net. It was in an industry where I had virtually no experience, but the comfort I felt made this position seem like the obvious direction I should take. I went from sorting mail, to learning to manage my father's business. During my time there I learned a great deal about the mental health industry and the subject in general. It also enabled me to identify my own mental health issues, face them, and ultimately overcome them.

Years went by and although I made strides in some areas of my own mental well-being, I still struggled financially, professionally, and personally. I was not just unfulfilled but felt like I was squandering my potential. It was a feeling that crept in and slowly took over my whole being. Any optimism I felt for my situation slowly dissipated, replaced with a hunger for stimulation. I endured this feeling for about four months before leaving the company to pursue something more challenging and satiating. Once I left the business, it would be six months before I started my new career. In other words, I had six months of self-reflection. In that time, I had to take a long look at myself and decide what type of person I wanted to be: someone content with achieving the bare minimum in life, or someone striving for more. I chose the latter.

Faith is a powerful tool. In hard times, it is a source of great strength. But like most tools, it gets worn over time, and occasionally needs to be sharpened. It can be difficult to hold onto and requires greater conviction as time presses on. My faith was tested in those six months. It was worn down and waning towards the end. Unemployment was starting to weigh heavily on my mind, and I was becoming a financial burden to those around me. And yet, I held onto that faith - faith in myself and in the inevitable improvement of my situation. I knew that if I just held on a little longer, I would be rewarded for my trust in the universe. Even though there were plenty of times when I wanted to give up and go back to easy, I kept my favorite mantra in mind, "Nothing worth having comes easy."

If it felt difficult, I knew I was on the right track. I knew what I was capable of, and I knew my time would come. And eventually it did in the form of an engineering position with a great company right in my own backyard, a job I received through my own efforts, which made it that much more gratifying. Knowing my own self-worth and displaying a positive nature was the key to them seeing my value.

Self-reflection is not only mentally cumbersome but can also be scary. But fear not, for we are all human, we all breathe the same air, and we all have to face ourselves in our respective way.

Some of us will have to overcome greater hardships than others. However, this does not mean that one person's struggle is greater than the next. It is all relative. What truly matters is not our mental hurdles, but that we overcome them in the end. And I promise you that no matter your hardship, you can rise above it. And when you do, you will be rewarded. When we accept our shortcomings, we can capitalize on our strengths and continuously improve on our weaknesses.

When dealing with the mental and emotional aspects of life, we must be our own *accountants*. And just like when we report our tax information to the IRS, we must be **honest with ourselves.** The IRS already has our tax information; they just allow us to report it to ensure we are staying honest about it. And when we are not, there are consequences. **Penalties** are the prices we must pay for not being honest.

Too many of us are not honest with ourselves. Therefore, we go looking for the wrong things in the wrong places. Even if we amass fame and fortune, if we are not honest with ourselves, then the time and effort spent gaining material wealth will be in vain. We could be surrounded by people and things, and still be as lonely as if we were sitting alone in an empty room. That void felt in the heart would remain.

Only when we are truly **honest**, will we finally learn and **know** ourselves and find where we fit in this world; and the type of company that is best for us to keep - those who bring out the best in us.

To reach that point in our lives, we must face not only who we are but what we are and how we feel. There are, inevitably, moments when we are disconnected from outside stimuli - moments when we are alone with our thoughts. Those moments may not be as frequent in this digital era, which is why it is more important to look for and utilize those moments of disconnection as the perfect occasions for self-reflection. When I am in the shower, or driving home from work, I occasionally turn off the radio and reflect on my day.

The minutes before falling asleep in bed are a good time to reflect on decisions made or emotions felt about the events of the day and to consider ways to improve tomorrow.

In sum, it may be useful to think about what you did during your day and how you felt about it. Perhaps you responded to a comment from a colleague; thinking back, you may have been caught off-guard, and your reply was not you at your wittiest. Not to worry; there will always be opportunities to "redeem" yourself. If you are like me, you are very hard on yourself when you don't have the best reply to a question or comment in the moment. This is not the end of the world, just another learning experience. In addition to our feelings about the day, it is critical to periodically reflect on where we are in life.

Are you where you thought you would be years or even days

ago? Do you enjoy where you are now? Are you on track to obtain your goals? If not, what will it take to get back on track?

These are all questions we must ask ourselves and answer truthfully. We won't get anywhere if we lie to ourselves. If we can't be honest with ourselves, then with whom can we be honest?

If we conclude that we are exactly where we are supposed to be, we must let go of the past and have faith in ourselves and the universe - that we will maintain our course and, in so doing, ensure that everything else around us falls into place. Along with faith, our responsibility is always to put forth the effort, keeping our foot on the proverbial pedal of life, continuing to press onward and upward.

***

Knowing the type of people that suit us best is only a portion of the battle. Kendrick Lamar summed it up perfectly in just four words, *"Sit down, be humble."*

Humility is key to creating an atmosphere other people will want to be around, which means taking the time to understand how others perceive our words and actions.

My fiancée and I used to have a roommate. "Chad" was new to the area and looking for work. He found employment at a local electronics store after working at a similar store for years near his former residence. That previous experience helped him get this new job but in a different position from his last one. Shortly after his employment began, he often came home angry or distraught. Some of his new co-workers had been giving him a hard time at work. Some would take his customers, refuse to assist him in certain processes, and exhibit other forms of passive aggression. From his account, it sounded like he had been targeted without reason. So, my fiancée and I would talk him through his stress and attempt to coach him on how to smooth things over with his apparent antagonists. He would then apply our advice and report on it the following day. His reports were seldom positive. We could not figure out why. As a new employee, nobody had any reason to give him a hard time. Or so we thought.

Over time, he revealed more of his character, which connected the dots. It became obvious that he was the architect of his own misery. We attempted to coach him in humility, but he chose to cling to his comfort zone in blaming others.

We soon realized all of his troubles began as soon as he got the job. He could not get a position equivalent to his previous one, and the position he did get felt like a demotion. Rather than be grateful, Chad was bitter about the job that he felt was somewhat beneath him. His bitterness was reflected in his temperament, which created an atmosphere of negativity and disdain - nobody wanted to be around him. Unfortunately, Chad could not see beyond his ego to the root cause of his mistreatment. Cue the vicious cycle of self-alienation. Chad came home every night and vented about his entire day to us. It did not matter what we were doing before he came home; as soon as he arrived, he expected us to pause our lives and allow him to pour out his frustrations. If we refused, we would also become antagonists in the "Chad Show." It never occurred to him that if he had just practiced a modicum of humility at his new job, his experience would have been completely different.

Humility means accepting that we are imperfect beings, have flaws and *always* have room for improvement. There isn't a single being walking this planet that is perfect. Claiming we are perfect means we no longer have anything to improve on; therefore, we no longer try. Growth ceases, replaced by stagnation. Humility allows us to see where our flaws exist and improve on them.

Pop culture and social media have influenced generation after generation to believe their needs fall into very specific categories. When we watch television or scroll through our media feeds, we see people flaunting material wealth, expensive cars, designer clothes, luxurious homes, and trips to exotic locations. While those are all good goals to set for ourselves - they should not be the sole focus upon which we build our character.

Blinded by these shallow assets, we miss out on deeper levels of fulfillment. We forget that Mental Equity is what sustains our minds and bodies. If we are too busy chasing the assets, we lose out on accumulating the Equity.

Abraham Maslow was a psychologist who specialized in humanism. His theory on human motivation suggests that people are driven by the urge to fulfill needs ranging from basic to complex. Those needs are: physiological, safety, social, esteem and at the peak, self-actualization (Motivation and Personality, 1954).

In the eternal quest to accumulate Mental Equity, Maslow's basic needs are just step 1. Fulfilling these needs must become part of our daily routine. And meeting one need can lead directly into the next.

So, eat. Eat heartily and healthily and get plenty of rest. We look better, feel better, and live longer when we meet our physiological needs.

In doing so, we can work and learn, secure employment and sustain independent living, meeting our need for safety.

So, now we are safe and secure in our healthy, employed existence. We will attract people - others who have met their basic needs or wish to. Either way, we have formed a social circle, increasing the likelihood of finding our romantic partner. Great! Social needs met, just like that!

Hard not to feel good about ourselves when we have a social circle of like-minded, healthy, happy people, who push us to be better. So, we strive for better living, and we help those around us achieve the same. Our friends and family make us feel good about ourselves and we naturally return the favor. Boom! Esteem needs met! It is almost like these needs fulfill themselves! And they should, this is our daily routine. Get used to it.

Now we are at the peak of our "pyramid" of needs. We are physically and mentally healthy. Without worrying about those needs, we are free to realize our true potential. We can nurture and build on the talent we always knew we had, turning it into a skill unique to us. And thus, self-actualization is realized!

As step one in the journey toward Mental Equity, we do not want to spend too much time determining if we have satisfied our basic and complex human needs. Instead, we can ask ourselves some very simple questions. The answers will determine if we are ready to accumulate Mental Equity.

Am I eating the appropriate quantity and quality?

Getting enough sleep?

Do I have a support system? A positive social network?

Do I feel safe? Secure? Stable? Physically? Mentally? Emotionally? Financially?

Do I believe in myself? Do I love myself? Are there those who love and appreciate me

Do I deserve all that I have?

Do I have all that I deserve?

Do I feel accomplished?

What are my goals?

Am I on track to meet them?

If the answer to any one of these questions is NO, then STOP!

Stop right there and before going any further, meet those needs and ensure the answers to each of those questions is YES.

Personally, I work on adding more structure to my life. I add reminders for multiple events in my calendar to promote good habits and discipline. This translates to ways where I feel more accomplished and work toward my goals with fewer backslides, keeping me on track to meet those goals.

Self-actualization, realizing our full potential, is not possible without satisfying every other basic and complex need. And by the way, there is no meeting all of these needs once and being done. There is no achieving self-actualization and moving on to the next thing. Each and every one of these needs and steps must be maintained and achieved over and over. It is part of our daily lives to ensure we continually reach our fullest potential. Mental Equity is not to be achieved. It is to be accumulated. And Life will not just hand it over. The universe *will* make us work for it. **EVERY. SINGLE. DAY.**

Because nothing worth having comes easy.

***

The beauty of our needs is that they are just that, our own

needs. It is all relative. Nobody can tell us when our needs are met except ourselves. Knowing ourselves means knowing our true needs, how to meet them, and when they are met. Neither social media, governments, nor politicians can tell us when our needs are met. The same is true for our friends and families. Praise for our accomplishments only has value when we believe it too! Only we know when we have enough rest, feel safe, feel loved, or accomplished.

The journey does not stop there. After all, just because we attain self-actualization does not mean we stop growing. In Maslow's later years, he believed another level existed beyond self-actualization. He referred to this new level as self-transcendence, which involves looking outside oneself and having a greater awareness and connection to people on a wider scale (Messerly, J.G., 2017, *Institute for Ethics and Emerging Technologies*). For now, strive to meet those needs!

PART TWO

RELATIONSHIPS

It is unbelievably important to surround ourselves with people who are "perfect" for us. I put *perfect* in quotations because perfection does not exist. What I mean by *perfect* is essentially, those who fit us like a jigsaw puzzle. They bring out our best selves, make us whole and allow us to do the same for them. This person does not have to be a significant other. We humans are social creatures. We cannot advance as a society living alone. We could not expand and grow as a species shutting out those around us. A person with no support system will find it difficult to navigate life and overcome its inevitable struggles.

Finding someone perfect for you could mean a friend, a mentor, a significant other, or even a pet. Who, or whatever they may be, will be exactly what you need when you find them (or they you).

We need stress outlets and opportunities to vent our frustrations. When Sally comes home from an unusually hard day at work, being greeted by her dog, Kojo, is much more beneficial to Sally's mental health than entering an empty domicile. In the latter instance, Sally may either let the loneliness overwhelm her, or try to ignore it, bottling it up and suppressing it.

Mental and physical health issues can manifest in numerous ways. Whether overcome with or suppressing our emotions, both can have detrimental effects on us and our surroundings. Allowing stress to fester in our minds and hearts has been known to cause real problems for our bodies. It can affect our appetites, motivation, attention to detail, and sleep patterns. All of which will negatively affect our bodies, and even increase the risk of us making silly mistakes that can have bigger consequences.

Knowing yourself is the key to recognizing those who compliment you. We have the awesome power to choose the company we keep. In doing so, we directly impact the very atmosphere we live in. In a way, we create our own reality.

When we find those people who complement our nature and enhance our character, we ought to hold onto them. Keep them in our lives so that we continue to be challenged to learn and grow. But do not forget to reciprocate! Otherwise, what reason do others have to keep us around?

We must not remain stagnant, having the right people in our lives is paramount to our success. Though many of us can get through and excel in life on our own, doing so via other people makes life much more complicated and exciting! The term, "It's not what you know but who you know," rings true.

Do not make the mistake of ignoring that gut feeling telling you that you have just met someone special. That someone could be a friend or even a lover. Either way, trust your feelings.

***

Terms like "follow your heart" and "go with your gut" were

coined for a reason. We are intuitive beings. Sometimes we have to clear our minds and listen to our inner voice. Too often, we over think our decisions. I do not know about you, but I am tired of hearing, "hindsight is 20/20".

Doubt, especially self-doubt, can undo all that we worked so hard to find. Trust that your gut will not steer you wrong. Remember that intuition I mentioned earlier? It comes with the big ol' brains floating around in our skulls. We all experience feelings of intuition, but many choose to ignore them. Continually doing so makes the feelings of intuition less and less apparent.

So, we must listen to our gut, opening our ears and our minds to the messages our bodies and subconsciouses are trying to send our conscious, over-thinking, overstimulated selves.

It helps to disconnect from the digital world at times. The constant stimulation from external sources creates a need for said stimulation in our brains. It can become an addiction. That is why we do our best thinking when in the shower, lying in bed at night, or even driving. I need an audio recorder when I'm in the shower because some of my best ideas originate while shampooing my hair.

When we are not staring at a screen, our brains can wander freely and generate organic, original thought - deducing situations in our minds without the help of outside forces. This disconnect takes practice, of course. The temptation of digital distractions lurks around every corner.

So, take 15 minutes out of your day and disconnect from any and all digital devices. Give your brain an open playground and see where it goes and what it does. It might just come up with something brilliant.

***

Temptation is very real and succumbing to it could cost us dearly. However, overcoming temptation breeds discipline.

We have all been tempted - faced with decisions that pertain to something good for us versus something not so good. Do I go to the gym, or eat a slice of cake? Do I go for a run after work, or watch one more episode of my new favorite TV show? And of course, one that hits home for me often, do I pick up takeout, or stay home and cook?

The answers to these questions may seem easy, but when faced with them in the moment, after a long, stressful day at work, choosing the option we know is better for us in the long run becomes that much more difficult. However, continually choosing the right option requires more effort but *will* reward us in the long run. After all, nothing worth having comes easy.

Now there is nothing wrong with indulging every once in a while. One does not have to eliminate the things in life that bring us relaxation or joy completely. After all, foods like cake or chocolate, are designed to elicit feelings of comfort and satisfaction. The brain needs that every once in a while.

And it is not just with food or lazy activities. Employing patience tends to be more rewarding than looking for shortcuts. Many of us have been stuck in traffic on our way home from a long day at work. We change lanes to get ahead of that slow mover, only to find another one waiting for us, or worse yet, there is an accident. Had we put on a little music, a podcast, or even an audiobook, and taken our time, we would most assuredly reach home safely, potentially a little more educated, and in a better mental space than when we left work.

Choosing the easy pleasures over the grueling effort may cost us dearly in the end. The same things that give us those pleasures can become our addiction and undoing. We end up craving those pleasures more and getting less from them. Instead of going straight for that dopamine-inducing treat, I reward myself with it. For example, I am currently studying Mandarin. So, I will only play a video game or watch TV after I have completed at least two lessons of Mandarin. Doing so, builds discipline and good habits in my daily routine. Methods like this can increase our resilience, confidence, self-esteem, and wellness simply by making the right choices.

The key is understanding that the universe is not out to get us; it is out to challenge us. The hurdles are not placed in our way to make us fall but to give us the opportunity to vault over them. We must try to rise to the occasion whenever adversity enters our lives and overcome it with courage and humility.

I know from personal experience that this is easier said than done. But with practice, it can become second nature. Remember, practice does not make perfect, but it makes better. And if we are truly honest with ourselves, we will also know when we deserve to indulge . . . every once in a while.

Now I won't pretend to know what you are thinking. But if I were reading this for the first time, I'd think, *damn, all of this sounds like a lot of work!* That's because it is!

Life is work. Hard work. All of the time. The point of Mental Equity is that all the hard work we put into life yields returns that make the hard work worthwhile. The goal is to ensure that we get as much, if not more, out of life than we put into it. The effort we put into knowing and loving ourselves and those around us must remain constant. Our lives and relationships cannot be put on auto-pilot; otherwise, we would sit there, watching the world go by.

Life requires maintenance. Our social needs, our self-esteem, and our careers require unabating effort. Doing right by our loved ones preserves our relationships with them, the effects on us, and vice versa. Be it a friendship or a romance, those relationships only stay strong when we invest our time in them. Even if it is just a quick call or a text message, we all desire to know someone else sees value in knowing us.

My fiancée and I have a core group of friends we met in the

Taekwondo club at Virginia Tech. It has been almost ten years since we graduated, and our little clique remains as bonded today as we were back in school. We maintain communication via a group text chain and occasional group video calls. We play games, share updates in our lives, plan trips, and share entertaining or useful information. We each acknowledge the importance of maintaining this friendship; therefore, the strength of our bond fails to wane.

***

We people need love in our hearts. In his book, "The Five Love Languages" (1990), psychologist Gary Chapman explains that we all have a "love tank" that, without love in our lives, can be drained completely, leaving us unfulfilled and even depressed. Our love language isn't just spoken by our significant others but also by friends and family. In fact, those who have known us the longest likely know our love language the best. Our responsibility is to communicate and reciprocate - especially for those we want to remain in our lives. Communicating our love language to that special person allows them to show us the kind of love that will fill our love tanks. This way, they are more confident in showing us love and we are receiving the love we desire and deserve. Everybody wins! And a likely bonus usually ends up being that a special person will share their love language with us. Without that open dialog, both parties are left to make assumptions, and we all know how that typically ends.

Balance in our relationships prevents everyone's "love tanks" from running empty, providing one more avenue to accumulate Mental Equity.

***

What is faith but trust in an unseen power? It could be our excuse not to feel responsible for the outcomes of our decisions or the situations that were out of our control in the first place.

Sometimes life has to get worse before it gets better. Thus, to achieve our goals, we place our faith outside ourselves and place it instead in the universe, trusting that whatever happens next happens exactly the way it is supposed to. We must have faith that the universe is propelling us toward our goals. It may not always look like it, but that is where faith comes into play.

Recently, I had a conversation with a close friend whom I will call Mark. Mark was always one of the nicest people I could remember meeting. His energy was consistently positive, and he was a joy to be around. Mark was the type of person who knew how to make you feel like the most important person in the room when you spoke to him. So, just out of curiosity, I asked Mark how he came to be this way. I wondered if it was just his nature or something he developed over time. The answer surprised me.

Mark shared with me that several years ago he learned his father had cancer. It metastasized at an alarming rate, and his family feared their patriarch might not have much time left. Rather than curse God, or beg the universe to save his father, Mark made a pledge. Mark promised to give himself over to the universe entirely, put his faith in it, and trust that whatever happened next, he would live with it. Mark also decided to devote his life to being a beacon of positivity and light, truly believing we can influence the world around us. Wanting to live in a world where the light shined bright, even when it rained, Mark decided he would be that light, trusting that if he remained his best self, the universe would reciprocate in kind. Do right by it and vice versa.

I am happy to report that Mark's father lived. Not only did he survive the cancer, but he beat it entirely and has been cancer-free ever since. I'm not saying Mark's pledge saved his father's life; Mark simply trusted the universe. He put his faith in it and believed his father was not meant to leave their family just yet. And what happened next was exactly what was supposed to happen. Mark wholeheartedly believes that, and so do I.

Examples like this make a case for putting our faith in the universe. If we make a habit of sending positive energy into the universe, we can trust that it will return that energy 100-fold. "What goes around, comes around," right?

I know it is easy to get stuck in that vicious cycle of uniformity. It is comfortable, it is safe, and we are in control. But we can grow so much more and faster when we dare to leave that cycle and venture into the unrevealed.

Have faith. You might just find your best self-waiting for you.

***

Let's talk about being present in the moment. Some of us can live in the moment without a care as to what has happened before or what will happen next. But MOST of us have to work every day and cannot live moment to moment. We work to survive and provide for our loved ones, making it much more important to know when and how to cherish those special moments.

We must recognize those moments and cherish them because they are so fleeting. It is both beautiful and tragic.

Every moment shared with another person is a point in time and space shared only by you and that individual. That moment will pass and never return. It is unique in its individuality, and only those in that moment will ever experience it. Hence the beauty and tragedy. Every moment is special, and we ought to treat it as such. Those fleeting moments make up our memories, which shape us mentally and emotionally.

It was in one of those cherished moments that I was struck with the idea to write this book. My girlfriend (now my fiancée) and I were enjoying a pleasant Saturday evening to ourselves. We tend to have very busy schedules, and this was a rare occurrence. We were lounging and watching television when a thought popped into my head. It was the realization of how well we were handling adulthood. We both have great jobs. We are not just financially stable but very secure. Our romantic relationship is healthy, and our "love tanks" are pretty full. We are both healthy, physically and mentally. Our pets are too. I took stock of all we had accumulated and achieved. Life is good, I thought. And we accomplished it together. It was a brief moment that I knew I had to cherish because tomorrow could easily change that, whether with a blessing or an issue.

At that moment, I knew I was experiencing a feeling we all deserve: all was well in our little corner of the universe. And we got there by doing right by it - working moments worth cherishing. It is in those moments that we accumulate Mental Equity. We are able to enjoy the fruits of our labor in simple yet meaningful ways. We did not need to be on an exotic beach, at the top of a mountain, or looking at a social media post with thousands of likes. We just had to be together, present in a life we built and maintained. Knowing that we are on the right path is worth just as much as reaching the destination. Even though we are still on the journey, we cannot forget to appreciate it.

I am willing to bet most of your fondest memories include other people. We share moments with the ones we love and cherish them for the rest of our lives.

But people will not gravitate towards each other without reason. I enjoy my fiancée because I love the way she treats me and vice versa. Same with my friends and co-workers.

The adage, "treat others the way you want to be treated," made sense when we were children, right? I did not want to be called names or shoved by others, so I refrained from doing it to others. As adults, we tend to project our moods. We tend to keep quiet if we do not want others to talk to us. If we are in the mood for debate, we look for argument. The problem with that concept is that everyone is different. We are all individuals, and we all respond to social interactions in our own unique way.

What we believe to be sincere and kind could be interpreted as the opposite if we are not careful. That is why it is important to communicate and avoid preconceived assumptions.

Let's look at a quick example:

While I worked in my dad's clinic, we had a client named John. John's father passed away several years ago. His friends gave him space, assuming he would want to be alone during his grieving process. With no one reaching out, John attempted to contact his best friend, who, conveniently, was too busy to hang out or chat. So, John went on to grieve alone, feeling rather lonely. John's grieving process was extended, making it more difficult for him to process his loss. One day, while at the grocery store, John ran into another friend, Gary. Gary reluctantly greeted John and asked how he was doing.

"Not well," John replied. "It's been difficult; I'm having a hard time processing it all."

"Would you like to grab a beer later?" Gary offered. John perked up a bit.

"Sure, I'd appreciate that," he answered. Later that evening, Gary stopped by John's place with a 6-pack, and they talked. Well, John did most of the talking, and Gary listened. Though it was a fairly depressing conversation, they both felt better by the end. John just needed someone to vent to, which assisted his healing process immensely, and Gary felt good knowing he was there for a friend in need.

A few years later, one of John's co-workers lost her mother. When he approached her in the break room, John attempted to talk to her about it, assuming it would likely work for the next person since it worked for him. John did most of the talking, trying to get her to share her feelings about her mother. Rather than pour them out, his coworker became frustrated with him and stormed off. John was confused by the entire encounter and left her alone from that point on. Later that week, she approached him and apologized. She explained that she typically likes to be alone, to grieve in peace, not wishing to share until she has had proper time to process. In turn, John also apologized, admitting he thought the opposite.

Communication is so much more than just talking. We speak in several different ways at the same time. It is very important to pay attention to body language and tone. Most people are not comfortable sharing their feelings out loud. So, we must listen to what people say and how they say it. You are not looking to catch people in a lie, but you want to know when someone is interested in your interaction or just trying to be polite until they find a way out. Do them (and yourself) a favor and read the signs. If their attention is clearly on something else while you are speaking, it is likely because they are trying to focus on something else. Save yourself a poor impression and grant their wish of solitude. It will show them that you are actually paying attention.

PART THREE

DUALITY

Merriam-Webster Dictionary defines *duality* as "the quality or state of having two different or opposite parts or elements." I believe we all exist in a state of duality due to the nature of our being and surroundings. But how does one find balance in such a state?

Positive and negative forces are constantly acting in the universe, which is how balance is maintained. Our goal is not to resist the forces when they affect our lives but to embrace them and respond in ways that maintain our inner peace. When we are out of balance, our lives can become destabilized. We begin to feel as though the universe is working against us. Losses hit us that much harder, and we over-correct, trying to gain more back. It is a lot like gambling. Several steady losses at the poker table make it very tempting to place larger bets in hopes of recouping those losses. It is sometimes better to be patient, have faith, and wait for the right time to make our move. Sometimes it is even better to cut our losses altogether, for our gains could be waiting for us elsewhere.

The key is understanding that the universe is not out to get us; it is out to challenge us. Because we do not enter life as our best selves, we need time and opportunities to practice making the best decisions. The universe repeatedly provides those opportunities. Therefore, we must rise to the occasion whenever adversity enters our lives; and overcome it with courage and humility. While easier said than done, with practice, it can become second nature.

We have all had those days that start negatively. Those days, we wake up "on the wrong side of the bed." We get out of bed, stub our toe or step on a child's toy (or dog toy). And we think the world is out to get us today. But in reality, it is our chance to prove that we can overcome what would just as easily be a "bad day."

Mental Equity cannot be accumulated without first finding balance in our lives. Like balancing a checkbook, life comes with gains and losses, positives and negatives.

***

Living as our best selves is guaranteed to attract the attention of those around us. People are naturally drawn to powerful, positive energy. Who would not want to remain in the presence of someone who makes us feel better about ourselves?

We must remain humble and grateful when we find ourselves at the center of attention. We may be on "cloud nine," but we must remain anchored by maintaining relationships with those who care about us and challenge us.

Remember, those who challenge us, balance us. There will be times when it gets too difficult to self-reflect, being distracted by everything else going on around us. Times like these require us to humble ourselves and rely on others who love and respect us enough to help keep us grounded, trusting that they have our best interests at heart.

Parents, close friends, and significant others are great examples of those who are not afraid to tell us when we are no longer staying true to ourselves. We should keep those relationships close and nurture them, because they will always hold us accountable for our actions.

***

Another obstacle encountered on this journey called life is how we deal with the past. Our past makes up a significant portion of who we are as individuals. It makes up our memories, both positive and negative. Therefore, it can be all too easy to get stuck in the days that are long gone.

While it is important to remember all that has come before, we must use the past to better navigate what is still to come. Dwelling on past blunders traps us in the feelings that afflicted us at that time, paralyzing us and preventing us from moving on. We can learn from our mistakes to avoid repeating them in the future, channeling any feelings of regret as motivation to forge a better path forward.

Remember, faith plays a vital role in our quest to accumulate Mental Equity. Failures tend to get the best of us, causing us to fret over the outcome. Faith has the power to propel us through stress caused by our errors. There is a place for everything and everything has a habit of finding its place. Have faith that the resolution to our gaffe will appear when it is supposed to. And in the meantime, we can continue living our best lives with the new knowledge gained from our most recent error.

***

When Mental Equity is first obtained, it can feel climactic. We have achieved a feeling of euphoria through sheer work and will. We have dedicated our efforts to being our best selves in every aspect of our lives. Our reward is a feeling that satiates our soul, which is beautiful and sad at that moment because it will pass. Yet, it must motivate us to accumulate those moments and sustain that euphoric feeling.

To do that, we must pursue higher states of being. Raise the bar higher in life and strive for it, raising it again and again, each time we meet our goals. Raising the bar may inspire others to do the same, creating a community with an atmosphere of yearning for higher living.

Sound good? I think so too. So, where do we start? How about higher education? I am not suggesting you pursue your Ph.D. in whatever topic interests you, but if it is in your wheelhouse, by all means, go for it. I am also aware that most people cannot afford to invest the time or the money in several years of grad school. We have families and careers we cannot up-end on a whim.

Therefore, I believe it is best to pursue higher education through other sources of knowledge. Look for ways to improve our knowledge base by reading books and articles with educational value. Soak in information from various sources, seeing how it is disseminated differently depending on the point of view of those reporting it. It is wise to take in all that we can with an unbiased mind and then judge how we choose to use the new information. But most importantly, learn! Learn more about our world and how to be a more productive and tactful citizen.

Learning more will promote a higher level of thought. As our knowledge base grows, so too will our character. We will not only thirst for more knowledge but also look for ways to apply it. Therein lies the higher sense of self and others. We will begin to hold ourselves to a higher standard. Why wouldn't we? At this point, we can confidently say we know better. When we actively seek out knowledge, it is more difficult to wallow in ignorance.

I find myself almost impulsively sharing what I learn. A higher sense of others and what they claim to believe drives me to ensure that those still ignorant of fact are at least exposed to it. In my day job, I've come across those who seek information from less reliable sources. Rather than challenge what they believe to be true and risk sending them into defensive mode, I encourage them to consider another perspective.

We must maintain a higher sense of ourselves and those around us. Not just in our immediate vicinity but around the world.

We are all on this journey together. This tiny rock, in the far reaches of space, is our home. Until someone comes out here and introduces themselves, we are all we have on this planet.

PART FOUR

FORCES OF NATURE

You may have heard the term "opposites attract." And it is very true, if you are a magnet. We are not magnets. We all move at a frequency unique to our individual selves; finding our opposite may expand our frequency but being with someone who complements us can enhance our frequency. That complementary person would be our "amplifier," someone who helps us build on our best qualities and improve the rest. Trying to find our amplifier will likely teach others to find their own. Couples that appear to have the perfect relationship appear as such because they are two people who found that they amplify each other. Healthy relationships between family, friends, and lovers set examples for our neighbors. We can inspire this type of positive behavior in one another.

The goal is to accumulate Mental Equity and rally our neighbors to do the same. We must become whole, complete, individual persons, who can connect with others as seamlessly as with our inner selves. That way, we can know and, in turn, find what it is in life that we truly want. We can realize our dreams using methods unique to who we are as individuals. And those around us will be more willing to help because we emanate authentic positivity, charging those around us with that energy - pure, humble honesty. These are traits to which people cannot help but be attracted.

The energy we put into the universe will come back to us tenfold. What we do then will have resounding effects on the very fabric of our reality. How we interact with those around us is key because the impact that we have on them sets the tone for how they will respond to us. Therefore, we directly affect our atmosphere in every setting. We must always keep this in mind. If we fail, we may find ourselves in a much darker world than we intended to create for ourselves. Hence my example of Chad in the earlier section.

***

Let us shift gears a little, going one step further into what I call "universal duality." Consider the four basic elements of our world: Earth, Water, Air, and Fire. I believe that their characteristics can be translated to those of human nature. Bear with me. It may be a stretch to some, but I think we can have a little fun with the idea.

Though we humans are complex creatures, our primary essence can be related to one of the four elements. While we all have layers of characteristics and a spectrum of emotions, our core nature is the focus here. It is who we are on the most fundamental level. Let's start with Earth.

"Solid as a rock" is a term we typically use when considering something to be reliable and sturdy. The nature of Earth is meant to be unyielding, yet it requires a great deal of effort to move earth in any direction it has not chosen on its own. For example, "moving mountains" is used when extremely difficult steps are taken to accomplish a task. Earth will not budge without the proper forces enacted on it, just like any one of us with an Earth nature.

Next, we have Water. Water "goes with the flow," so to speak. The very nature of Water is nurturing and healing, but also willing to move in any direction pressed upon it. Those with a water nature tend to be more easy-going facilitators, in a way, and very caring.

Then there is Air. If Water goes with the flow, Air is the flow. Those with an Air nature can be considered free-spirited at heart. Air is a nature that creates its own direction, whether or not others follow it. Those of this nature will happily sway others in their direction, but never forcefully. They are more likely to make suggestions than give orders.

Finally, we have Fire. Some think of Fire as destructive, raging anger. But, if we look at the root of this potent emotion, we will often find a true passion for that over which a fiery person would find worthy of erupting. It takes courage to emote such passion in a way that draws attention to them. A fiery nature will happily lead the charge toward a cause they feel strongly about and attempt to rally others behind them.

I have some theories I would like to share about how I believe these elements will interact with one another. By elements, I mean human nature relating to those elements. If we take these elements one step further, we can argue that some are more synergistic than others. The idea is to build synergy with one another rather than cancel each other out.

Again, these are fun theories to consider regarding the primary nature of ourselves and our neighbors. It is unlikely that we are one single elemental nature. As complex beings, we are more precisely different combinations of each nature, leaning more heavily toward some than others.

Earlier, we discussed finding the amplifier for our nature, someone who builds on our best qualities. Someone who brings out the best in us and vice versa. Someone with whom we can build *synergy*.

Merriam-Webster defines *synergy* as a mutually advantageous conjunction or compatibility of distinct business participants or elements (such as resources or efforts).

Look for synergy in the company you keep. Family, friends, and lovers ought to be people with whom we produce a greater effect together than we would when apart. Sound about right?

If we take the four elements one step further, we can argue that some are more synergistic together than others. For the first example, let's look at Water and Earth. Adding Earth to Water helps water rise. Earth accommodates Water, giving it shape, so those with unyielding personalities will help give direction to those who prefer to "go with the flow." In other words, a stalwart attitude can freely remain so when coupled with a personality more willing to follow than attempt to lead.

So, then let's look at how our final two elements might interact. Remember the last time you went camping and tried to light a fire? As soon as you get a few embers going, what is the first thing you might attempt to do next? Blow on it. Giving Fire some air will help it grow. Fire needs Air to sustain and expand. I would argue the same can be said for the aforementioned natures.

Now, we have covered all four elements and their guaranteed amplifiers, but there are more combinations of personalities that will inevitably meet. There could be friends with personalities that may not be perfect amplifiers but still get along. Let's theorize on how those others might interact.

The free-spirited nature of Air can rarely move the unyielding nature of Earth. Rather than expend all of its energy, Air will likely flow right over Earth and into another direction, usually the path of least resistance. In other words, the free-spirited type won't spend much time trying to move a stubborn individual. Instead, they will just go around.

Air and Water are two natures that I believe can be easily misconstrued. While Water tends to "go with the flow," Air is "the flow." Water's easy-going nature looks a lot like Air's free spirit. However, Water needs direction from another while Air always has its own direction in mind.

Fire and Earth can be mistaken for each other. Fire's uncompromising passion looks like Earth's indomitable spirit, and an unyielding Earth may easily douse Fire's passion. On the other hand, if Fire burns hot enough and long enough, Earth could melt and give way under the intensity.

Now on to Fire and Water. I think we can all imagine how this combination will play out. I believe it is safe to assume they will cancel each other out. Water is typically unaffected by Fire's intensity. Instead, Water likely challenges Fire, resulting in less potency and more reflection. After all, Water is a natural mirror.

There are more combinations of these four elements. Feel free to theorize on your own. If you come up with some great ideas of your own, please reach out. I'll happily entertain the ideas.

At the end of the day, only we can truly know our element. Yet, the only way to discover our primary nature is by being completely honest with ourselves. We return to our first section, Know Yourself. We can converse with our inner voice, meditate, and accept who we are. These are just a few ways to accomplish self-reflection and self-discovery. There is no good or bad in nature, only energy that needs to be projected in a positive direction.

PART FIVE

MENTAL EQUITY

As mentioned before, self-actualization leads directly to Mental Equity. It is **balance**. It is finding balance in our lives and seeing the **beauty** in that balance. The point is to find that balance and amplify it. We can then begin to, and continually accumulate Mental Equity.

Remember, Mental Equity is happiness gained from the things we obtain through the work we put in to acquire them. We go to work to earn money. With that money, we pay our bills and save what we have left to buy items or experiences. Whatever we choose to put our hard-earned money towards ought to give us a sense of joy and fulfillment. If that is not the case, then we are not earning Mental Equity, and we should immediately rethink our priorities. Working without accumulating Mental Equity will leave our lives and our minds unbalanced and unfulfilled.

The goal is to find balance on our unbalanced planet. As our home revolves around the Sun, it tilts on its axis (middle school science class stuff, I know. Stay with me here, there is a point I'm getting to). As the world tilts, our atmosphere changes, as does our mood, from positive to negative, like the magnetic poles. The goal here is to maintain our balanced selves as the world tilts. It will become more difficult to remain balanced as the climate advances to one we favor less.

If you are not a fan of the cold, it is even more important to focus on maintaining your balance during the winter. One may not enjoy Spring due to immense allergic reactions to pollen.

Therefore, one must stay balanced as mother nature begins to bloom again. The same is true for any other season.

Mental Equity helps us determine if we are on the right path. It confirms for us when we are on said path. Then, it gives us direction for where to go. Once on the right track, our work enables us to obtain real fulfillment. Fulfillment is the sign that we are on the right path. It is then that we begin to accumulate Mental Equity. It is meant to help us break any negative cycles we may be stuck in and commit ourselves to a positive cycle once we have corrected our course. Jumping on the right path is only step one. Once we find our way, the real journey to self-actualization begins!

Huzzah! We have stayed the course and achieved every basic and complex human need on Maslow's pyramid. Our potential is realized, and we are complete. Yet, the journey is far from over. If we assume we have already won the game of Life because we have achieved self-actualization, then we are mistaken. The primary focus must turn outward to our neighbors. Of course, we must continue to look inward, remembering mentally to check in with ourselves regularly. Only when we truly find ourselves will we start to see our neighbors. And when I say "see" our neighbors, I mean understand them. Understanding *who* they are is just as important as understanding *why* they are.

Mental Equity is continuous improvement in Life. Improving our lives and the lives around us will undoubtedly build Mental Equity.

In the song, *Shot to the Heart*, Hip hop artist Rick Ross once said, "How many people you bless, is how you measure success." And he's not wrong. Blessings come in many forms; most do not require official, religious titles or mass wealth. Something as simple as a smile, or a compliment, can brighten anyone's day, even when they are at their darkest.

PART SIX

CLOSING THOUGHTS

Mental Equity is a goal we all strive for, whether we know it or not. I wrote this book in a manner that was open to interpretation because there is no single formula that will work for everyone. While we are all looking for *something*, we are not all looking for the *same thing*. The only way I could tailor this to every single person is if I met every single person. While I would love the opportunity, it just is not realistic.

So, I wrote this to help you, the reader, begin to think about yourself on a deeper level. My goal is to help you connect with your inner-most self so that you can form deeper connections with those around you. Because what are we all looking for?

Our purpose.

Connection.

Where we fit in this life.

The role we are meant to play in this universe.

These are the questions we all ask ourselves throughout our lives. We have the answers; we just don't know where to look. Many of us look for it in other people, in vices, or in anything that gives us a semblance of gratification - although the answer was inside us all along. All we have to do is turn our focus inward and listen. There it is, clear as day, waiting to be found, waiting to flourish.

You, dear reader, you are what you have been looking for. Find yourself, know yourself, stay true to yourself, and everything else will fall into place. The rest is **Mental Equity**.

www.ingramcontent.com/pod-product-compliance
Lightning Source LLC
Chambersburg PA
CBHW071935020426

42331CB00010B/2882